Dedication

I am so proud of my four children and son in law. Christo, Elaine, Jake, Sonia, and Soraya. Your continued success is motivating and a source of Great pride.

Acknowledgment

I appreciate the many students and staff from the Pascep community education program at Temple University. I especially would like to say thank you to the founder Ms. Annie Hyman and the Director Ms. Muriel Feelings. I had a career for 30 plus years as a Financial

Advisor. My twenty years of teaching the Personal Finance course for Pascep was Fantastic.

Introduction

Generally when people think of debt reduction there are five ways they consider.

1) Consolidate: you are going to combine some debts with others possibly lowering your monthly payment.
2) Transfer: Very similar you could eliminate some interest charges but still have to make your payments.
3) Negotiate: Talk with your creditors to get the interest rate down or forgive some of the debt.

4) Bankruptcy: Either eliminating paying anything back or getting a 60 month schedule to make the payments.
5) Management: You focus on managing your payments until the debt is gone.

   This book is using the management method.

I was talking to my daughter Soraya about managing the payments for a car she was considering buying and she said "I can handle it but I will have to do it from the muscle." I had never heard that term and asked her to explain. She said that it meant she would have work hard. I was amused by the phrase and now writing this book I feel that it is an appropriate title for my approach to Debt Management.

You will get out of debt by using this information but you will be doing it "From the Muscle".

Chapter 1

Cash Management

Finding the Money

I always outline three distinct financial situations.

1) The ideal situation is when your income is considerably higher than your expenses. The gap or difference is what you can use to reach your financial goals.
2) The second situation is when there is a narrow gap between income

and expenses but the slightest hiccup in your finances would be a problem.

3) The third situation is when expenses are exceeding income. This situation is where people tend to use credit to cover the expenses that are above their income. The problem is when you have to continue using credit month after month to maintain your expenses. You should only use credit up to what you can pay off in 30 days. Otherwise you are going to go deeper in debt every month.

One word of caution after the debt is eliminated without vigilance you can still end up in a bad place. I remember when Bill Clinton was

President and he raised the income tax rate on people making over $100,000 per year. Those folks were saying why is he coming after us we don't have any money. If you make more and spend more guess what? Your financial situation will be the same. Instead of the Chevrolet you drive the lexus, still a car note. Instead of an attached home you have a single, you still have a mortgage. Instead of shopping off the rack for suits you get them tailored made, still just clothes. Etc.

We can correct situation 2 and three but we have to complete an exercise first that you should find insightful.

You will need to fill out a Cash Flow sheet for 3 months.

I did not say a budget. This step is to make sure you know

where your money is going. Many times I find when people reach financial difficulty they just are not doing good accounting on their spending. By doing the cash flow statements for three months you can know exactly where your money is being spent. Once you have an accurate idea of where money is being spent there will be some areas you will want to change that you can change with a decision on your part. This is how we are going to "find the money" to help you manage your debt.

I have included three pages for you to list all expenses that you have. List expected and actual in the spaces provided. This will allow you to see what you thought you were doing as well as what you are actually doing. Once this is done you will find that there is money that has not been covered. Many times people say the bills are too much. But what you will find out is, it is not the fixed bills like mortgages or electric bills etc. Instead it is in the area of variable expenses. These areas of spending are often without a record of expense. So as you fill out the cash flow statement pay special attention to this area.

Here are examples of what I have found over the years working with clients in this area.

1) Eating out for lunch: After filling out the cash flow statement with a client and reviewing the details we realized he was eating out for lunch almost every day. He happened to work in New York City and at that time he was spending about $15 a day for lunch. So $15 a day 5 days is $75 for 4 weeks is $300 per month. Did he really want to spend $300 a month for lunch ? The solution, don't eat out every day.

2) Socializing: This client was hiding his car in a garage so it wouldn't get repossed when we met. After filling out and reviewing the cash flow statement there was about $500 per month missing. So I asked him to walk me through what he did

when he received his pay. He said he would cash his check and go to his favorite local bar run the bar twice and head home. He explained that run the bar meant that he was buying everyone at the bar a drink. So if 20 people were there at the bar and the drink was $3 that was $60 twice is a $120 per week a total of $480 per month. So the solution: Direct deposit the check and only run the bar once. I always wondered how many people had heard about him coming on Fridays at a certain time and buying everyone 2 drinks ?(hmmm)

3) Taking a walk: I went through a cash flow statement with a client because all of a sudden money was

tight and she could not see what had changed. We did the same walk through as I had with the "cheers" guy. We found that she had switched parking locations from a few blocks away to across the street from her job. Across the street was $15 a day while a few blocks away was $5. So $10 per day difference is $50 per week $200 per month. Solution Put back on the walking shoes for that couple of blocks.

4) Here is one of my favorites The lottery play in the box. A person playing the lottery in box play for .50.

Someone who plays 12 numbers day and night is playing $12 per day. In a month's time they have paid over

$360 in that month. The most they could have won based on the numbers they were playing was $200 in some numbers $100. So boxed numbers were a terrible bet, guaranteed to lose 80% on your money if you happened to "win" once that month. A $160 loss. Solution don't play boxed lottery bets, and save $360 per month.

5) Over saving: I had a couple who were making out pretty good financially but they couldn't seem to find the money to buy a car and afford a car note. I found out that they were putting away $600 per month in an art account. This was an account in case they found a piece of art work they wanted to buy.

Solution Split the account put $200 per month in the art account and use the rest toward a car note.

I could go on but my point is that until you seriously look at where you are spending your money you can't be sure what you can do "from the muscle".

So take some time and use the cash flow sheets. I am going to assume that the decision you make allows you to "find" $150 per month.

Cash Flow outline month 1

Fixed Expenses	Variable Expenses
	Projected/Actual
Rent /	Food
Mortgage /	Transportation
Electric /	Personal care
Telephone /	Donations
Water /	Repairs
Heat	Entertainment
Life Insurance /	Recreation
Home owners insurance cleaning /	Laundry/Dry
Health Insurance /	Travel /vacation
Child care /	Clothing

_____ Lunches
/

_____ Saving/investments

_____ Gifts
/

Repairs
/

Installment Debt: Department stores credit cards loans

Bill 1 _____ Bill 2_____ Bill 3 _____

Bill 4_____Bill 5_____Bill 6_____

Bill 7_____Bill 8_____Bill 9_____

Cash Flow Outline Month 2

Fixed Expenses	Variable Expenses
	Projected/Actual

Rent /

Mortgage /

Electric /

Telephone /

Water /

Heat /

Life Insurance /

Home owners insurance /

Health Insurance /

Food

Transportation

Personal care

Donations

Repairs

Entertainment

Recreation

Laundry/Dry cleaning

Travel /vacation

Child care   Clothing
/

_____   Lunches
/

_____
Savings/Investments   /

_____   Gifts
/

                                                              Repairs
/

Installment Debt: Department stores credit cards loans

Bill 1 _____ Bill 2 _____ Bill 3 _____

Bill 4 _____ Bill 5 _____ Bill 6 _____

Bill 7 _____ Bill 8 _____ Bill 9 _____

Cash Flow Outline Month 3

Fixed Expenses	Variable Expenses
	Projected/Actual

Fixed Expenses	Variable Expenses
Rent /	Food
Mortgage /	Transportation
Electric /	Personal care
Telephone /	Donations
Water /	Repairs
Heat	Entertainment
Life Insurance /	Recreation
Home owners insurance /	Laundry/Dry cleaning
Health Insurance /	Travel /vacation
Child care /	Clothing

_____   Lunches
/

_____   Savings/investments

_____   Gifts
/

                                        Repairs
/

Installment Debt: Department stores credit cards loans

Bill 1 _____Bill 2_____ Bill 3 _____

Bill 4_____Bill 5_____Bill 6_____

Bill 7_____Bill 8_____Bill 9_____

Chapter 2

Debt Reduction

To start your debt reduction program you have to list every bill that you have that has an end to it. That does not include Utility bills, groceries, Insurances, etcetera. It does include credit cards, department stores, car notes, college loans, Mortgages, etcetera. Once you have the bills listed to eliminate, list the due date for each bill in the next column. In the third column list the total owed on each bill. In the fourth column list the monthly payment due. In the fifth column use a calculator and divide the third column by the fourth column. So you are dividing the total owed by the monthly payment. This is the amount that goes in the Fifth column.

Now it is time to evaluate your debt priorities. Notice I didn't mention the interest rate to make an evaluation. In this program what is most important for the evaluation is out of all the bills which one has the highest monthly payment but the lowest balance. Go through your list and go bill by bill numbering them 1 through the last one based on that factor only. Highest monthly payment lowest balance. Put the priority number you come up with in the sixth column. The bill that you list as number one is the bill that you will be focused on paying off first.

Now in chapter one you hopefully found some money you are committing to your debt reduction program. All of that found money goes on that number one priority bill. So you have two parts that you are paying on that bill. The regular payment due plus the found money amount. After whatever number of months it takes to pay off priority bill number one you will have better cash flow, the amount that you were paying on that bill that was due plus the found money amount. Here comes the discipline. Because you have better cash flow you don't go splurge on a new car note or whatever else while you still have other debt to pay off. **Key Point All money in the**

debt program STAYS in the debt program until all debt is paid off.

Now you place the monies from priority bill 1 plus the found money and the amount normally due on priority bill 2 all on that bill. You continue this until bill 2 Is paid off. Everything now goes on priority bill 3. This continues until ALL debt is paid off.

Here is an example of how this debt reduction plan looks in action. Page listing all the debts and prioritized. Second page showing how this system helps to reduce the debt. The biggest bill of $7,000 with a monthly payment of $240 would normally had taken 29 months, only takes 20 . Now after all debt is paid this situation leaves a financial situation with an extra $590 per month. With that level of extra money the only bills you probably could not handle through a few months of cash flow are a car note, college loans and a mortgage. Those are areas for the next chapter.

Debt Reduction in action

Priority order, Highest monthly payment lowest balance

Total	monthly	# Of mths	1	2	3	4
$165	$25	7	$165 x			
$400	$20	20		$195		
$630	$29	22			$195 x	
$700	$25	28				$224
$780	$20	39				
$1,360	$61	22				
$7,000	$240	29				
$11,535	$440					

$150	$150	$150	$150	$150	$150	$150	$150
$25	$25	$25	$25	$25	$25	$25	$25
$175	$20	$20	$20	$20	$20	$20	$20
	$195	$29	$29	$29	$29	$29	$29
		$224	$224	$25	$25	$25	$25
				$249	$20	$20	$20
					$269	$61	$61
						$330	$330
							$570

With an extra $150 per month towards debt reduction the $11,535 in debt is paid off in 20 months.
At that point you would have an extra $570 per month in extra cash.

Debt Reduction worksheet

bill	due date	total	payment	#of mths	priority

bill	due date	total	payment	#of mths	priority

Major Debt

The biggest difference with major debt is the amount of money involved and the loan period for the debt.

The major three I want to focus on are

1) Car notes 2-7 years.
2) College loans 2-15 years
3) Mortgages 20-35 years

All three of these loans have scary end amounts of money that you will pay out over the time period. However they are all open end loans, which allows you to pay all or a **portion** of the loan ahead of that payment schedule.

Let's take a look at the car loan. I mentioned my daughter earlier buying a car and having a car note. Well by the time we finished with the car salesman and the finance manager we had a 72 month payment schedule with a 3 year bumper to bumper warranty. Now if we keep to the 72 month schedule the $14,000 loan will cost $22,824.

Instead this car will be paid off in less than 3 years that's why we settled with the 3 year bumper to bumper warranty. In her case we could have put $2,000 more down to the lower the monthly payment on the car note. But that would not have a big difference in the monthly payment. Instead we look at her total debt and payment schedule. There is one bill of $166 with four payments left (priority bill 1) Credit card bill $85 per month with 6 payments (priority bill 2) and a third bill of $1600 at $100 per month(priority bill 3). So with $842 of the $2,000 available we eliminate bill 1 and 2 freeing up cash flow of $251 per month. That is a better use of the $842 than using the money to lower the monthly payment of the car note. The $842 on the car note might have saved $40 per month. That $251 plus $100 of bill 3 means she will be able to pay off bill 3 in less than 5 months. So after five months she can put an extra $350 per month against the car note. Three fifty per month for 20 months is $7,000 of **principal payments only** against the loan. What about the rest of the $2,000? After the first payment is made a separate check is written for **principal payment only** of $1,100. From the beginning she will not be paying interest on $14,100 but instead on $13,000. So instead of paying $22,824 she will pay approximately $17,000, saving $5,000.

With any of these three long term debts you can make a principal payment paying down the amount you owe ahead of the set schedule. I suggest you always make this principal payment totally separate from your regular payment. Check afterwards that it was applied as a principal payment. I have had more than one occasion when a person thought they were getting ahead but they didn't say this was a principal payment and the money was accounted for by the company as loan payments.

It is easier to see what a difference this makes by reviewing a mortgage amortization schedule. Many times people wonder why does a house cost three times the price that they thought they were paying for it. The mortgage company is collecting the interest on the loan first over that 30 years. A page of an amortization schedule of a $100,000 mortgage with a 7.5 interest rate is very revealing. We are just looking at principal and interest payments only. Out of $700 paid each month in the beginning only $74 is going towards paying back the original $100,000 borrowed. In this situation on a mortgage of $100,000 after 48 payments, four years of payments and $33,600 paid in, only $4,600 of that is applied on the loan. The change in interest charged for that entire 48 months is only $25. Always request an amortization schedule when you purchase a home. Than you can exactly see how much of your monthly payment is going towards interest and how much is going towards the principal of the loan.

It is entirely up to you but if you plan on staying in your home for 20-30 years, You should seriously consider making some principal payments early in the mortgage.

I had a client who had just purchased her home.

So my house warming gift was a card with a money order made

payable to her mortgage company equal to 3 principal payments of her mortgage. That cost me less than $200.

I haven't mentioned college loans but they work the same way as car loans and mortgages. You can pay ahead of schedule. Graduating your cash flow from college student to working adult should be quite an increase. If you take that opportunity to use a good portion of that new "found money" to concentrate on debt reduction the college loans should be less of a burden to pay off.

I have used the program many times over the years to help clients get a grip on their finances. Because with the debt out of the way could concentrate other financial goals. These include saving for college educations, building a retirement nest egg, making charitable donations or other goals. I hope this book has been helpful to you for your financial security by eliminating your debt concerns.

www.ingramcontent.com/pod-product-compliance
Lightning Source LLC
Chambersburg PA
CBHW071202240526
45470CB00017B/1244